KU-132-419

Secrets Of Art

Elizabeth Newbery

Belitha Press

First published in Great Britain in 2001 by
Belitha Press Limited
London House, Great Eastern Wharf
Parkgate Road, London SW11 4NQ

Editors: Claire Edwards, Kate Phelps
Designer: Jane Horne
Picture researcher: Diana Morris
Consultant: Erika Langmuir
Education consultant: Sue Lacey

ISBN 1 84138 305 8

British Library Cataloguing-in-Publication Data for
this book is available from the British Library.

Printed in Hong Kong

Picture acknowledgements

Cover:
Bonhams, London/Bridgeman Art Library: front cover tr. Graphische
Sammlung Albertina/Bridgeman Art Library: front cover br. Mattioli
Collection, Milan/Bridgeman Art Library: front cover cr. Museum of Fine
Arts, Houston, Texas/Bridgeman Art Library: front cover c © Klee
Foundation/DACS London 2001. Craig Tuttle/Stockmarket/Corbis: front
cover l.
Arts Council Collection of Great Britain/Bridgeman Art Library: back cover
© Les Hériteurs Matisse/DACS London 2001.

Inside:
Arts Council Collection of Great Britain/Bridgeman Art Library: 15tr © Les
Hériteurs Matisse/DACS London 2001. Ashmolean Museum,
Oxford/Bridgeman Art Library: 16r. Bonhams, London/Bridgeman Art
Library: 13l, 29tl. Brooklyn Museum, New York/Bridgeman Art Library:
1b,19t. Burnstein Collection/Corbis: 25tr © Les Hériteurs Matisse/DACS
London 2001. Christies, London/Bridgeman Art Library: 23bl © DACS
London 2001. Geoffrey Clements/Private Collection/Corbis: 15bl © Dedalus
Foundation/DACS London 2001. Jack Fields/Corbis: 13r. Freer Gallery, The
Smithsonian/Bridgeman Art Library: 9b. Elizabeth Fritsch/Sara Morris/Crafts
Council: 17tr © Elizabeth Fritsch. Gemaldegalerie, Dresden/Bridgeman Art
Library: 27t. Giraudon/Bridgeman Art Library: 19br, 29br. Graphische
Sammlung Albertina/Bridgeman Art Library: 10b, 28b. David Lees/Corbis:
16bl © Henry Moore Foundation 2001. Mattioli Collection, Milan/Bridgeman
Art Library: 25br. Musée D'Orsay, Paris/Giraudon/Bridgeman Art
Library:27b. Museum of Fine Arts, Houston, Texas/Bridgeman Art Library:
7b © DACS London 2001, 14br © Klee Foundation/DACS London 2001.
National Gallery, London/Bridgeman Art Library: 5b. National Gallery of
Scotland/Bridgeman Art Library: 7t © Succession Picasso/DACS London
2001, 8c © DACS London 2001. Norton Simon Collection, Pasadena,
CA/Bridgeman Art Library: 11cr. Palazzo de Te, Mantua/Bridgeman Art
Library: 22b. Pictor International: 5tr, 14tr. Picture Press/Corbis: 4bl. Private
Collection/Bridgeman Art Library: 9t © Henry Moore Foundation 2001, 24tr
© DACS London 2001. Rijksmuseum Vincent Van Gogh,
Amsterdam/Bridgeman Art Library: 3t, 24br. St Louis Art Museum,
Missouri/Bridgeman Art Library: 26c. Santa Maria del Popolo,
Rome/Bridgeman Art Library: 21. Photo Richard Sargent: 11bl © Marilyn
Levine. Alan Schein/Stockmarket/Corbis: 17br. Tretyakov Gallery,
Moscow/Bridgeman Art Library: 23br © DACS London 2001. Craig
Tuttle/Stockmarket/Corbis: 4r. Victoria & Albert Museum,
London/Bridgeman Art Library: 12b, 23tl. Wallace Collection,
London/Bridgeman Art Library: 20cr, 20b. Peter Willi/Ashikaga Museum,
Japan/Bridgeman Art Library: 18b. Peter Willi/Louvre,Paris/Bridgeman Art
Library: 11tl. Michael S Yamashita/Corbis: 2b, 6b.

Every attempt has been made to clear copyrights but should there be
inadvertent omissions please apply to the publisher for rectification.

**Some of the more unfamiliar words used
in this book are explained in the glossary
on pages 30 and 31.**

Contents

Have you ever looked at a piece of art and wondered why you like it? Perhaps you are curious as to why your eyes are drawn to a certain part of a painting? Or why you want to touch a sculpture?

In the know

Artists have secret ways of making us look at works of art and holding our attention. They can make our mouths water or make our flesh creep. They can frighten or worry us, make us laugh or cry. And all by using line, pattern, texture, colour and light in certain ways! In order to discover how they do it, we must learn more about the tricks of their trade.

◀ *Touch me!*
Texture tells us how something feels. In everyday life, it tells us when to touch and when not to touch. This chick covered in soft, downy feathers makes us want to stroke it. But would you feel the same about a big, hairy spider?

◀ Colour signals
Colour gives out messages. Some creatures are brightly coloured to attract a mate. Others, such as wasps with their yellow-and-black stripes, send out warning messages – don't touch or I'll sting!

Follow the lines ▶
Lines lead our eyes to certain points. Your eyes will follow this line of trees whether you want them to or not!

▲ The Graham Children by William Hogarth, 1742
In the eighteenth century, William Hogarth was a well-known painter. He was asked to paint this portrait by the children's wealthy father. Hogarth has painted their clothes in such a way that we can imagine what they would feel like if we touched them. Shadowy lines suggest the shape of the room. And he has used colour, light and shade to make us believe these children are almost alive.

Drawing lines is one of the simplest ways of expressing ourselves – and one of the oldest too. Some of the earliest images ever found are lines carved and painted on rock.

Lines can be thin or thick, bold or delicate, straight or wavy, dark or light, continuous or broken. They can be painted, drawn, built, printed, cut out or stuck on. And you can use anything to make lines, from chalk to chisels. We use lines every day to make letters and numbers, maps and directions, symbols and signs. Artists use lines to express a great variety of ideas in many different ways. They use them to describe different types of shapes, feelings and moods, texture, movement and space.

Drop a

▲ *Garden in Zuiho-in Monastery, Kyoto, Japan*
In this Japanese garden, fresh lines are raked through the sand every day. The lines represent waves and ripples on water.

Bacchanal by Pablo Picasso, 1959
At first glance, you may not think this linocut is especially linear (made up of lines). But look carefully. Can you spot outlines round shapes? Or lines which express movement? Or single and overlapping lines? The artist cut lines into a block of lino to make the print.

line!

Number 6 by Jackson Pollock, 1949
This tangled mesh of lines was created by pouring and dribbling paint from a can. The artist, Jackson Pollock, was interested in paint for itself and what it could do, rather than what he could paint with it. He didn't intend these lines to hint, suggest or represent anything at all.

Not all lines are there to be seen! Sometimes artists just want to suggest or hint at lines. You may not realize they are even there. But why do artists do this?

Hidden

Sometimes artists may want us to focus our attention on a particular spot or hint at the shape of objects, edges, height, depth, space and movement. Artists know that they don't have to draw lines to make us see them. They can suggest lines with a row of objects, a string of highlights in the same colour or just a raised arm. They can even hint at lines with the marks made with a brush as Vincent van Gogh did in his painting *Wheatfield with crows* on page 24.

▲ *Poplars on the Epte by Claude Monet, 1891*
This artist has suggested lines to hint at space and distance. Look how he draws our eyes into the distance with trees that follow the curve of the river. He hints at the edge of the riverbank with a broken line. The tree trunks and their reflections emphasize height.

▲ *Shelter Drawing by Henry Moore, 1941*
Here, the artist describes the shape of sleeping
bodies with lines disguised as folds of cloth.
Look closely and you will see he has also used
fine, criss-crossed lines (called crosshatching)
to show the curve of the limbs.

lines

◄ *Nocturne, Blue and Gold: Valparaiso*
by James Abbott McNeill Whistler, 1866
James Whistler has used tiny dots of yellow and
orange to represent lights on boats moored in a
harbour at night. Although the dots are very small
they 'join up' to suggest a string of boats on the
far side of the harbour with the shadowy line of
the coastline beyond.

Texture is how something feels. But artists can make something look as if it has texture even if it hasn't really. Or they can use paint and other materials to make the surface have real texture.

Touchy-feely

Texture is one of the ways in which an artist controls the way we react to a painting. So artists can make us imagine that we know how something feels, smells, sounds and tastes. They can make us react so strongly that we don't have to touch to feel. Texture can also describe the way in which materials are used. For example, paint can be squeezed straight out of a tube or painted on with coarse brushes and used as texture. Some artists mix paint with other materials such as sand to make another kind of surface.

▶ *Hare by Albrecht Dürer, 1502*
This painting appeals to our sense of touch. The artist has captured every hair on the animal's body from its soft ears, quivering whiskers and velvety nose to the long, thick fur on its back. Does this picture make you want to stroke the hare?

Still life with a Ham by Floris van Schooten, seventeenth century
This painting of ham, cheese and bread set out on a table appeals to our sense of taste. The artist has painted the food to look so real it almost makes our mouths water!

Johan's Jacket by Marilyn Levine, 1990
Some artists like to fool us with texture. This coat looks as though it is made of leather. It's really made of clay!

The Mulberry Tree by Vincent van Gogh, 1889
The artist has used paint squeezed straight out of the tube. He might even have spread it on with a knife or his fingers. The tree doesn't look as real as the ham or the hare. But do you think the rough paint helps us to imagine the sound of the wind rustling through the leaves?

Do you have some clothes with patterns on them?
If you look closely you will see that the pattern is usually
made up of one shape or shapes repeated many times.

Fancy pattern

Patterns can be woven,
printed, painted,
embroidered, cut out and
stuck on. They can decorate
anything from bedclothes to
baskets. They can make things
more attractive to use, have
special meanings, make things
more valuable and even show
off special skills! But artists
can use pattern in other
ways too. They can use it to
describe different surfaces and
textures, movement and ideas.

◀ *Unknown man by*
Nicholas Hilliard, 1588
This man is dressed
in the latest fashion in
the time of Elizabeth I.
His doublet (a type
of short jacket) is
made of a repeating
pattern of bands
of black and
white fabric
joined together.
Notice that even
the buttons are
decorated.

Dragonfly lampshade
by Louis Comfort Tiffany, about 1900
Louis Comfort Tiffany was an American artist and craftsman who owned a glassworks. He experimented with blending colours and inventing new ways of making ornamental glass. He liked to decorate the glassware with shapes based on nature such as insects, flowers and birds.

Cloth on sale in Guatemala, Central America ▲
All countries have folk artists. They are ordinary people who make and decorate everyday things with traditional patterns and colours handed down from one generation to another. The figures on these pieces of cloth on sale in a market show the colourful traditional dress of Guatemala and the way in which women carry goods.

Not all shapes make patterns – they can stand alone too. Shapes can be two-dimensional and flat or three-dimensional with height, width and depth.

Shaping

These two pages look at flat shapes; those which have width and height but no depth. You can make flat shapes by drawing or painting them, by cutting them out or sticking them on. You can create them with stencils or by printing them. Flat shapes can be natural, like an animal, geometric, like a square or abstract, like the shapes in the print by Robert Motherwell on page 15. Shapes can even give out messages – a skull and cross bones means danger, a crown means a king or queen. Perhaps you can think of others.

▶ *Mariam's House by Paul Klee, 1928*
Paul Klee has painted flat, geometric shapes to describe his friend's house. The shapes may remind you of roofs, doors, windows, streets and even a map of the town. But the artist doesn't invite you to explore the three-dimensional space inside and around the houses or the town.

◄ Shapes with meaning
These arrow shapes tell us that we must follow certain directions. They mean the same thing wherever you live in the world.

up!

The Horse, the Rider and the Clown ▲
by Henri Matisse, 1947
When Henri Matisse was old and ill, he was unable to paint. So instead he cut out flat shapes from painted paper and stuck them on to a background. The shapes in this picture represent his memories of a circus he saw when he was younger.

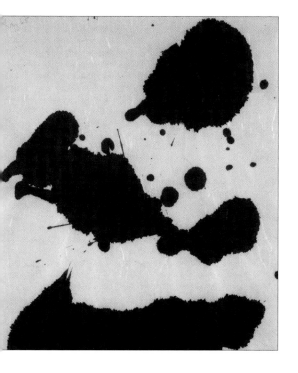

◄ Abstract print
by Robert Motherwell, 1965
At first this picture seems very simple. But if you look hard you will see that it is much more complicated. For example, do you see big black shapes splattered on to a white background? Or one large white shape with black shapes torn out of it?

Three-dimensional shapes (called form) have height, width and depth. Most things in this world have form, for example, chairs, books, computers and you!

Deep

Some forms are solid and some are hollow. Both help to reveal the structure of the world around us. Artists such as sculptors and potters only make works of art with form. (There's no such thing as sculpture or pots without form!) Form can be found in nature, for example, as an apple or a tree. It can be geometric like a football or abstract like the sculpture below.

◀ *Oval with points by Henry Moore, 1972* When you look at sculpture you need to move round it to see it from all angles. Henry Moore often made sculptures with holes that you could see through. They give his sculpture an extra feeling of space and depth.

Pithos with octopus design from Knossos, Crete, about 1450 BC
This storage jar was made about 3,500 years ago, but the potter knew about making a form look attractive. Notice how the octopus' tentacles emphasize the form of the pot.

Over The Edge – Wave of Particles by Elizabeth Fritsch, 1994
This potter attempted the impossible! She has used pattern to try to make a three-dimensional form look two-dimensional (flat). How well do you think she has succeeded?

shapes

Skyscrapers, New York
Architects build things with form. Buildings, such as these skyscrapers in New York, are all good examples of geometric forms. Interior designers work with form too. They work with the hollow spaces inside buildings.

What happens when painters who paint on flat surfaces (two dimensions) want to show height, width and depth (three dimensions)? The answer is they have to use special effects.

Looking real

When painters want us to believe that a picture looks like real life, they have to show form, volume, space and distance. We have to see the air around trees in a landscape, a bowl sitting comfortably on a table or people with their feet firmly on the ground. There are several ways in which artists can make space look real. They can use overlapping shapes, objects and people drawn in proportion to their surroundings as well as colour, light and shade.

▶ *Good Omen by Yoshinobu Yokoyama, twentieth century* This Japanese artist shows distance by making trees on the horizon lighter and mistier. The trees closer to us are darker.

▲ *The Peaceable Kingdom by Edward Hicks, about 1840*
On the left of this painting the river disappears into the distance. People are drawn in proportion to each other and their surroundings. This side looks 'real'. On the right, the children in the foreground are smaller than the animals in the background so there is no sense of distance or scale. This side doesn't look real.

▶ *Harvesting grapes. From the Tomb of Nakht, Egypt, twentieth dynasty (1186–1071 BC)*
The Ancient Egyptians believed in life after death. They weren't interested in showing space to make things look real. They wanted to show daily life in as much detail as possible so that the dead could go on living as before. They painted things from the angle at which they appear most clearly. For example, people don't stand like this but we immediately recognize what they are doing.

Perspective is the mathematical way of showing distance and scale. In Europe, painters have used perspective since the Middle Ages to make paintings look more realistic.

Real views

Perspective is the best known way of making flat surfaces look three-dimensional. It involves lines that meet at vanishing points – the place in the distance, such as the horizon, where two or more parallel lines seem to meet (see diagram right). It's easier to imagine railway tracks that seem to meet on the horizon. The point at which they meet is called the vanishing point.

Vanishing point

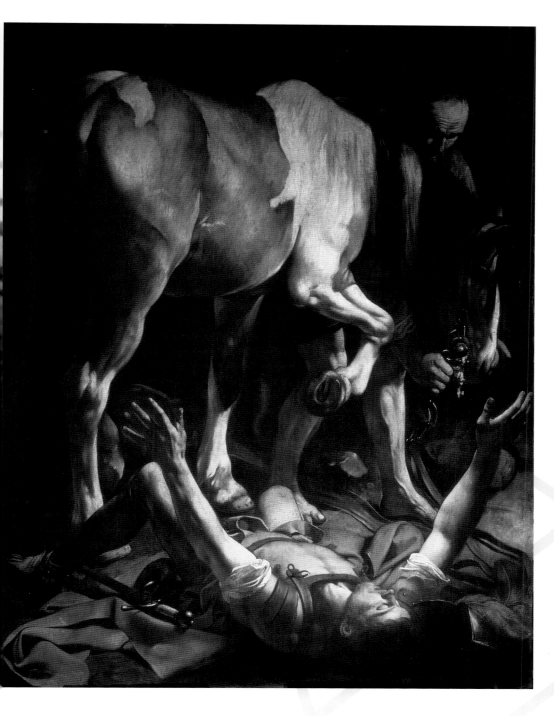

◀ *The Conversion of St Paul by Michelangelo Caravaggio, 1601*
St Paul lies on the ground. His head is painted large, his arms long and his legs very short. He would look very odd if he was really like this! Caravaggio had to draw St Paul in this way to make him look as though he was lying down. This effect is called foreshortening.

◀ *The Riva degli Schiavoni by Antonio Canaletto, 1740–45*
Antonio Canaletto used a piece of equipment called a camera obscura to help him make drawings of buildings in perspective. It was a box with a small hole in one side through which light entered. The light formed an image of the scene on a piece of paper, which the artist traced off. He used these drawings to make his final paintings.

Many artists like breaking rules and showing space in unusual ways. Others are interested in playing conjuring tricks with space – now you see it, now you don't!

Space

Many artists have painted things that tricked people into thinking they were real. This trick is called trompe l'oeil which is French for 'to fool the eye'. Trompe l'oeil was popular in Ancient Greece and Rome. A Greek artist called Zeuxis is supposed to have painted grapes so real that birds tried to peck them! During the Renaissance trompe l'oeil became popular in Europe. Whole rooms were painted with false perspective. In them artists even painted pretend windows and doors through which people seemed to be looking or passing.

▶ *The Gods of Olympus by Giulio Romano, 1528*
Giulio Romano was well known for trompe l'oeil. He painted this fresco on the ceiling of an Italian palace. Where does the ceiling begin and end? What is painted and what is actually there?

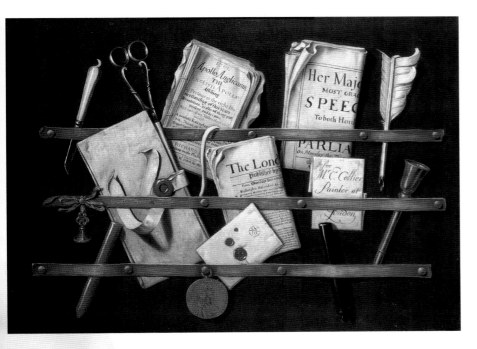

▲ *Trompe L'oeil Composition by Edwaert Collier, 1701*
Trompe l'oeil of still-life subjects like this one are more difficult to make convincing. The viewer can inspect them at close quarters, unlike a ceiling.

▼ *The Fiddler by Marc Chagall, 1920*
Marc Chagall often showed things floating in space, which may seem odd at first. Chagall was Jewish and grew up in Russia. Many of his paintings are memories of his childhood and of Russian-Jewish folk tales. He painted them in a child-like way, as though they were dreams. Now that you know this, does the way he used space seem less odd?

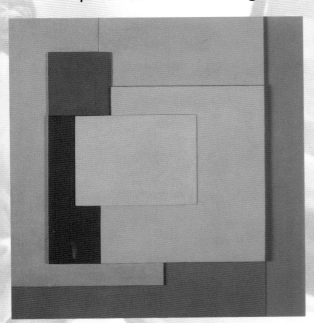

◄ *Painted relief by Ben Nicholson, 1940*
Ben Nicholson liked playing games with space. Look hard at these shapes. Do you see how some of them appear to come forwards and others go back?

games

How do you make a still painting or sculpture look as though it's moving? Artists have tried to solve this problem in different ways since prehistoric times.

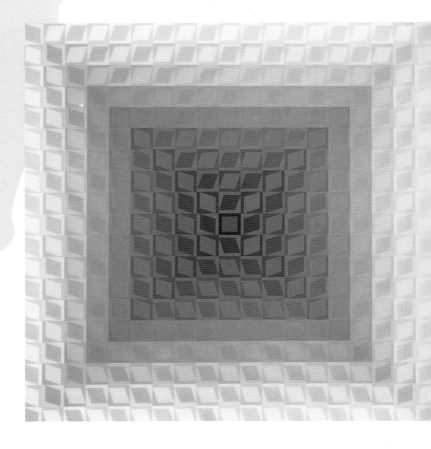

Into

Some artists show movement by capturing frozen moments in time. Others use devices to trick the eye into thinking a picture is moving. This is called optical movement. Some sculptors make sculptures that change shape as the viewer moves round them, like the example by Henry Moore on page 16. Others make sculptures that actually move. This is known as kinetic art.

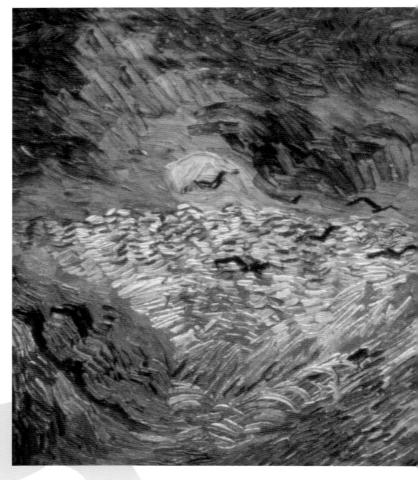

▶ *Wheatfield with crows by Vincent van Gogh, 1890*
Painters can suggest movement by using paint in a particular way. This artist has used thick paint to make the wheat sway in the wind, clouds scurry overhead and crows swirl around.

◀ *Composition by Victor Vasarely, 1960*
If you stare at this painting for a few seconds
it will appear to move! The artist has created
optical movement with lines, shapes and colours
to trick you into thinking the picture is moving.

Dance by Henri Matisse, 1910 ▶
The sense of movement is so powerful in this
painting that it looks as though the figures are
actually dancing. Notice how the pattern of limbs
and bodies shows the direction of movement.

action

▼ *Unique Forms
of Continuity in Space
by Umberto Boccioni, 1913*
Umberto Boccioni was a Futurist.
Futurists were a group of artists
who lived at the beginning of the
twentieth century. They were
interested in speed, machines and
city life. This sculpture doesn't
move, but it gives the
impression of someone
striding ahead at great
speed. The legs
even appear to
have wings – as
though someone
is battling against
the wind.

We have looked at the secrets and tricks of the trade separately. Now we look at how artists use them together to make a complete picture. The design of a whole work of art is called composition.

Clued up

Artists use composition to make you look at and feel about a work of art in certain ways. They may highlight part of a painting to focus your attention on it. Or place things in a certain order, to tell a story. Movement, colour and balance are used to make paintings look more pleasing or disturbing. By searching for clues to the way an artist wants you to look, you will usually discover works of art are more complicated than you first thought.

▲ *Raftsmen playing cards*
by George Caleb Bingham, 1847
George Caleb Bingham painted lots of pictures of frontier life in North America. This painting shows men on a raft on the Missouri River. As in the painting by Jan Vermeer, the action takes place in the centre. But Bingham has chosen to focus your attention with perspective, which draws your eye to the men.

Girl reading at an open window
by Jan Vermeer, 1659

This girl is reading a letter – but what does it say? Look how Vermeer makes us curious. He has placed her in the centre of the picture and highlighted her face. Our eyes are drawn first to her face and then to the letter. The curtain is arranged so that we seem to be spying on the girl. A shadowy reflection of another person in the window is also seen watching the girl.

The Snake Charmer
by Henri Rousseau, 1907

Who is the snake charmer? What else lurks in the jungle? Henri Rousseau has created a mysterious picture by placing the snake charmer to the left of the centre. He has filled the painting with a strange greenish light to give an eerie feeling.

About the artists

➤ *George Caleb Bingham* was born in Virginia, USA, in 1811 and died in 1879. He is best known for his scenes of frontier life.

➤ *Umberto Boccioni* was born in Reggio Calabria, Italy, in 1882 and died 1916. He was one of the first Futurists and one of the most enthusiastic members of the group.

➤ *Antonio Canaletto* was born in Venice, Italy, in 1697 and died in 1768. He first worked as a scene painter. Later, he became famous for his paintings of Venice.

➤ *Michelangelo Merisi da Caravaggio* was born in Caravaggio, Italy, in about 1571 and died in 1610. Caravaggio had a temper and was often in fights.

➤ *Marc Chagall* was born in Vitebsk in Russia in 1887 and died in 1985. He was a deeply religious man and many of his paintings are about religious subjects.

➤ *Edwaert Collier* was a Dutch artist born about 1640 who died in 1710. He painted many trompe l'oeil paintings like *Composition*.

➤ *Albrecht Dürer* was born in Nuremberg, Germany, in 1471 and died in 1528. Dürer was interested in exotic animals. On a visit to see a dead whale, he caught a fever and died.

➤ *Elizabeth Fritsch* was born in Wales in 1940. Her pots are not made on a potter's wheel but are built up and decorated by hand.

➤ *Giulio Romano* was born in Rome, Italy, about 1499 and died in 1546. His greatest works were frescos and painted rooms.

➤ *Vincent van Gogh* was born in Groot-Zundert, the Netherlands, in 1853 and died in 1890. He was a troubled man who felt strongly about things. He suffered from mental illness and shot himself.

➤ *Edward Hicks* was born in Attleborough (now Langhorne), USA, in about 1780 and died in 1849. He became a Quaker minister and all his paintings have religious meanings.

➤ *Nicholas Hilliard* was born in Exeter, England, in 1547 and died in 1619. He was trained by a goldsmith. Most of his paintings are jewel-like miniatures.

➤ *William Hogarth* was born in London, England, in 1697 and died there in 1764. He is best known for pictures that poked fun at the way some people lived.

➤ *Paul Klee* was born in Münchenbuchsee, Switzerland, in 1879 and died in 1940. His paintings are often funny and he was very fond of children's art.

➤ *Marilyn Levine* is an American artist who makes works of art in clay.

➤ *Henri Matisse* was born in Le Cateau, France, in 1869 and died in 1954. He was a painter, sculptor and designer, as well as a book illustrator.

➤ *Claude Monet* was born in Paris, France, in 1840 and died in 1926. In the 1860s, he and others showed their work at an exhibition and became known as the Impressionists after Monet's painting entitled *Impression: Sunrise*.

➤ *Henry Moore* was born in Castleford, England, in 1898 and died in 1986. He was one of the most important English sculptors of the twentieth century.

➤ *Robert Motherwell* was born in Aberdeen, USA, in 1915 and died in 1991. He was a philosopher (someone who studies thought) before becoming a painter. Motherwell believed that unless it had thought behind it, art was just decoration.

➤ *Ben Nicholson* was born in Denham, England, in 1894 and died in 1982. Most of his paintings are based on geometric shapes.

➤ *Pablo Picasso* was born in Malaga, Spain, in 1881 and died in France in 1973. During his long life he worked in many different mediums such as pottery, sculpture and printing.

➤ *Jackson Pollock* was born in Cody, USA, in 1912 and died in 1956. He was famous for his paintings made by pouring, dripping and splattering paint on to a giant canvas laid on the floor.

➤ *Henri Rousseau* was born in Laval, France, in 1844 and died in 1910. He was called 'le Douanier' (a customs officer) because he began to paint as a hobby while working for the customs office.

➤ *Floris van Schooten* was born in Delft, the Netherlands, about 1585 and died sometime after 1665.

➤ *Louis Comfort Tiffany* was born in the USA in 1848 and died in 1933. He was a painter, designer, glassmaker and jeweller.

➤ *Victor Vasarely* was born in Pécs, Hungary, in 1908. He was the first person to make Op Art.

➤ *Jan Vermeer* was born in Delft in the Netherlands in 1632 and died in 1675. He is one of the greatest of all Dutch artists.

➤ *James Abbott McNeill Whistler* was born in Lowell, USA, in 1834 and died in 1903. He was interested in the links between art and music.

➤ *Yoshinobu Yokoyama* is a Japanese artist.

Things to do

Make lines *pages 6–7*
Try making lines with different things dipped in ink or paint, such as a stick, a length of string or a small piece of sponge. What sort of lines do they make?

Rubbing textures *pages 10–11*
Collect several objects with different textures, for example, a rough piece of wood, a pebble, a comb and a basket. Then lay a piece of thin paper on top (layout paper from art shops is good) and rub the surface of the paper with a thick crayon. You will get rubbings of the objects on the paper.

Spotting shapes *pages 14–15*
Spot how many shapes that give out messages you can see in your local high street.

Paint a picture map *pages 14–15*
Describe where you live like Paul Klee did. Make a map of your house, street or even your school. You could use one colour for friends, another for neighbours and another for family. Or one colour for houses you don't like and another for ones you do like.

Emphasizing shapes *pages 16–17*
Paint a plastic flowerpot with white emulsion. Using a dark colour, paint a pattern to emphasize the shape of the flowerpot.

Glossary

abstract Art that does not necessarily show things as we see them in real life.

balance The feeling when parts of a work of art fit well together.

blend To mix together.

camera obscura An instrument used for drawing perspective.

composition The arrangement of all the parts of a painting.

crosshatching Shading created by fine, criss-crossed lines.

doublet A close-fitting padded jacket worn by men from the fourteenth to seventeenth centuries.

embroidered Decoration made with needles and thread on to cloth.

emphasize To exaggerate.

form Three-dimensional shape.

foreshortening A way of drawing objects or people pointing away from the viewer so that they appear to be three-dimensional.

Futurists A group of artists interested in speed, machines and city life.

geometric Mathematical shapes such as squares, triangles or circles.

highlight A way of drawing your attention to something.

horizon The line where the land or sea seems to meet the sky.

kinetic art Sculpture that moves.

landscape A painting of scenery.

line A continuous mark.

linear Something which is mainly made up of lines.

linocut Prints made by cutting into lino, inked then printed.

miniature A very small picture, often a portrait.

Op Art Art based on optical effects made to trick the eye.

optical movement Pattern or colour made to look as though it is moving.

pattern Repeating shapes or shapes which fit together to make another shape.

perspective A mathematical way of showing three-dimensions.

pithos A storage jar used in Ancient Greece.

print A way of making an image by inking a surface and pressing it on to another surface.

proportion The way one object, person or part is seen next to another.

Renaissance A time in history that began in fifteenth-century Italy. It inspired many new ideas and inventions that spread across Europe. Many great works of art were created during the Renaissance.

sculpture A work of art in three dimensions.

shape A pattern which has a line drawn round the outside.

special effects Things that happen which are different from any other kind.

stencil A cut-out shape.

still life A painting of a group of objects.

texture The way we respond to a work of art through touch; the surface of a work of art.

three-dimensional Shapes that have height, width and depth.

trompe l'oeil Art made to trick the eye.

two-dimensional Shapes that have height and width but no depth. They are flat.

vanishing point The point where two lines seem to meet on the horizon.

volume The amount of space filled by something.

woven Something that is made by weaving soft materials in and out.

Index